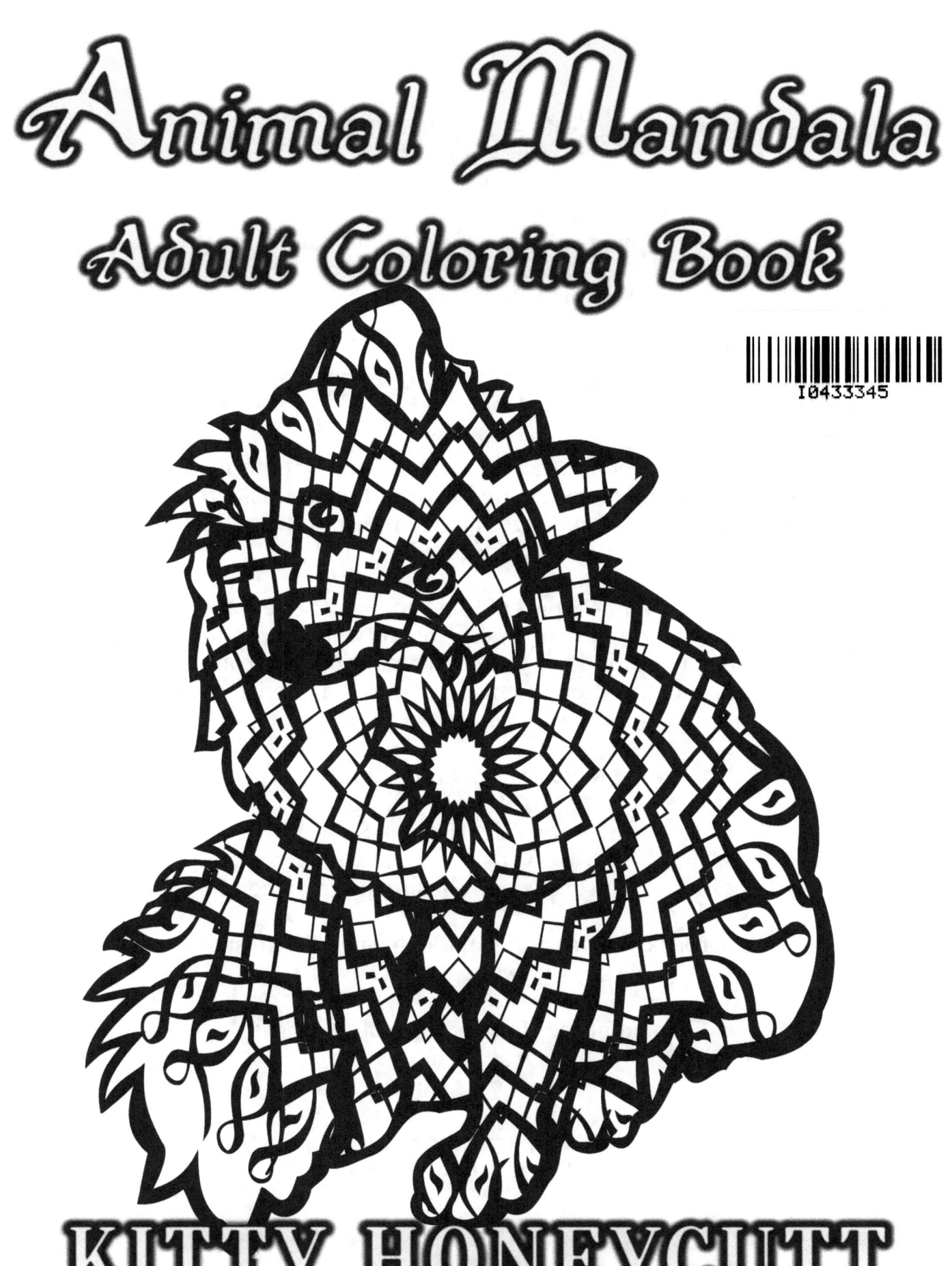

ANIMAL MANDALA
By
Kitty Honeycutt
Copyright © Kitty Honeycutt 2017
Cover Copyright © Ravenswood Publishing 2017
Published by Gaia's Essence
(An Imprint of Ravenswood Publishing)

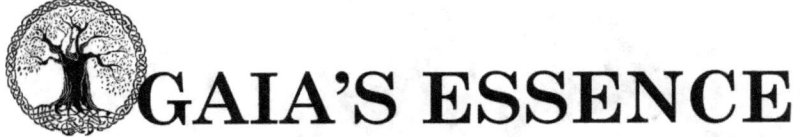

GAIA'S ESSENCE

This book is a work of non-fiction created entirely for entertainment purposes. All pictures were created with combinations of free clip art from various sources. All images are creations of the author and are copyrighted.

All rights reserved. No part of this book may be reproduced or transmitted in any form or by any means whatsoever, including photocopying, recording or by any information storage and retrieval system, without written permission from the publisher and/or author.

Ravenswood Publishing
1275 Baptist Chapel Rd.
Autryville, NC 28318
http://www.ravenswoodpublishing.com
Email: RavenswoodPublishing@gmail.com

Paperback orders can be made through Createspace
http://www.createspace.com

Printed in the United States of American
First Edition
10 9 8 7 6 5 4 3 2 1

ISBN-13: 978-1979322065
ISBN-10: 1979322066

This book is dedicated to my amazing daughter, Rhianna Bullard. Her love for animals knows no bounds. She is an inspiration to everyone she meets.

I love you baby duck!

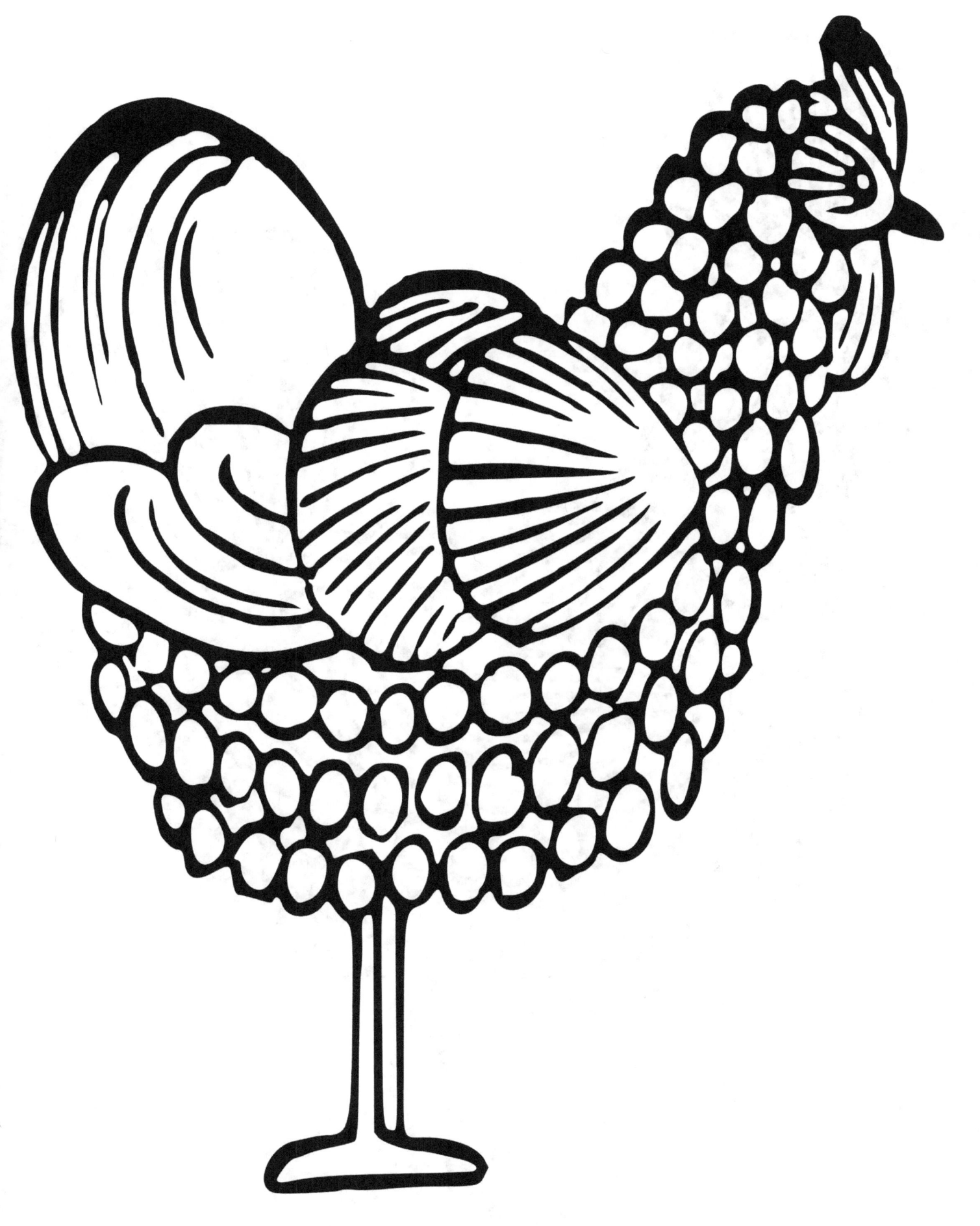

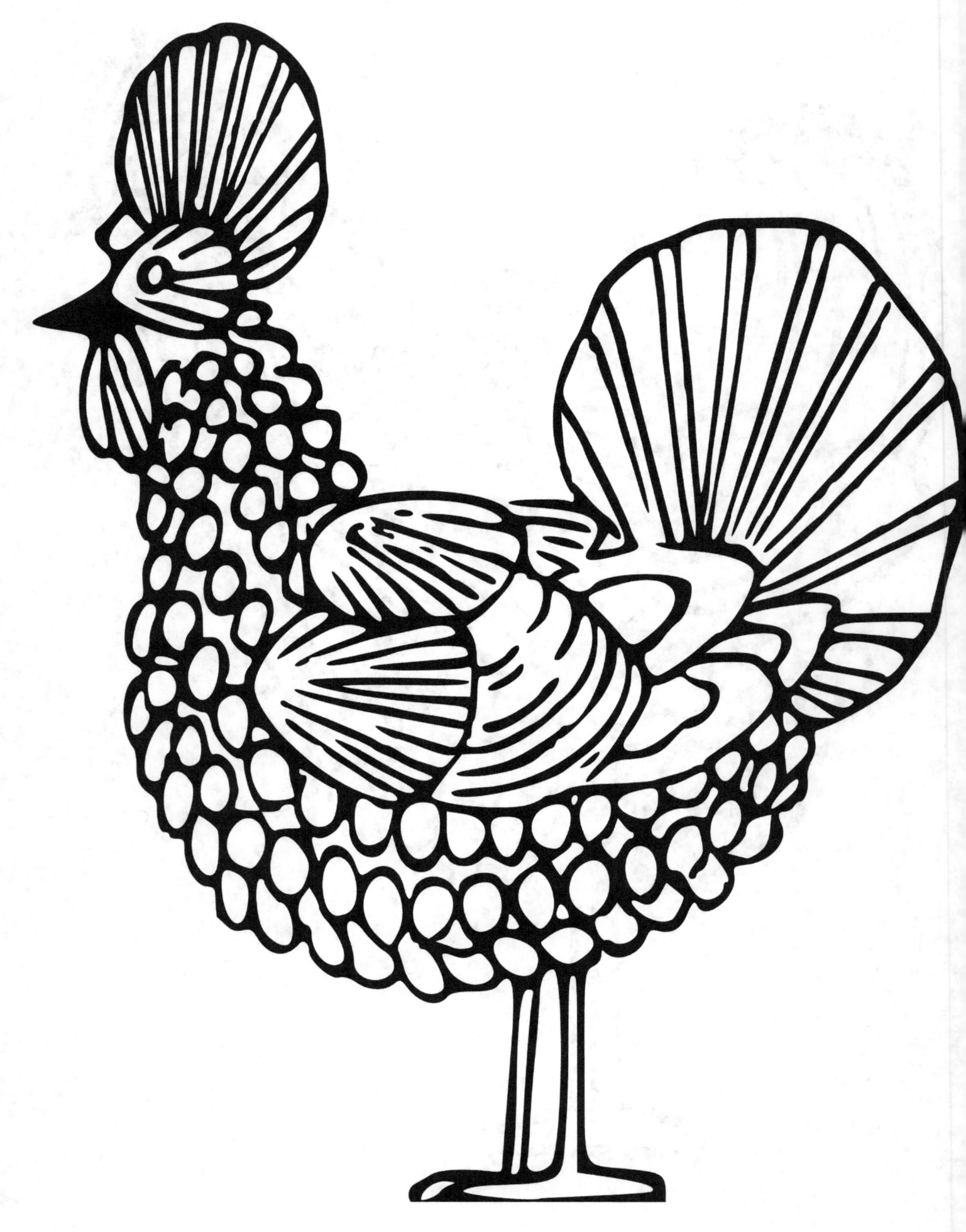

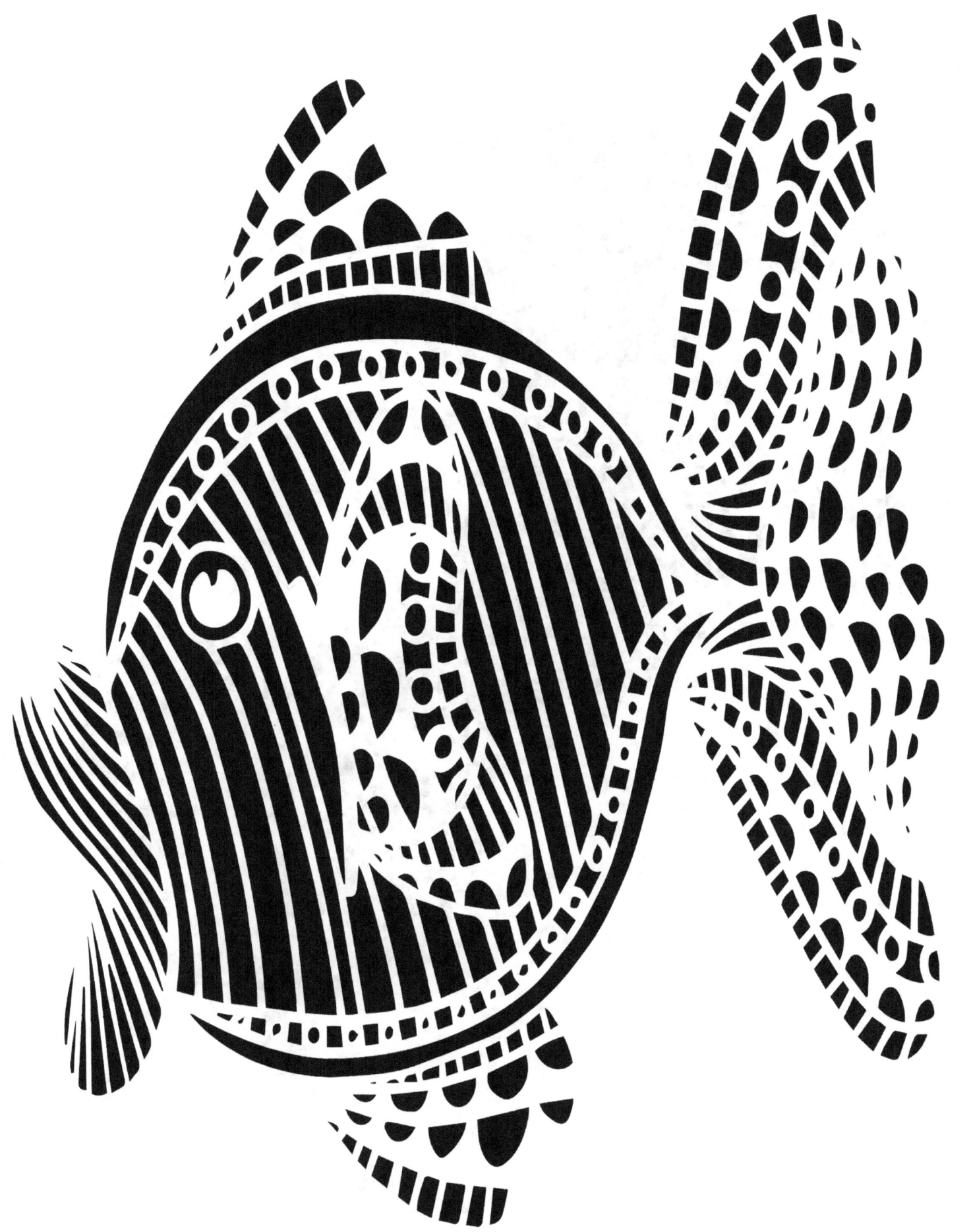

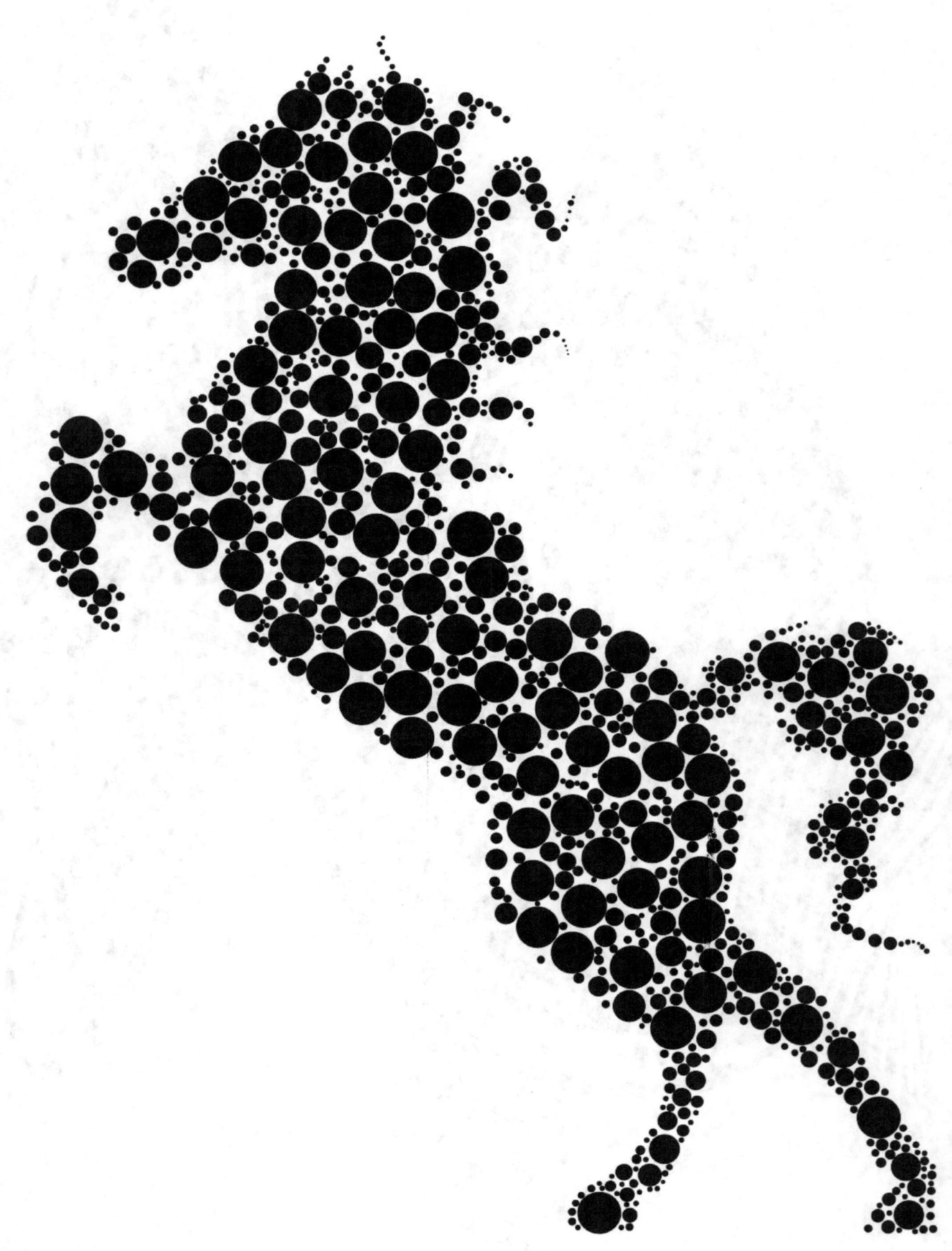

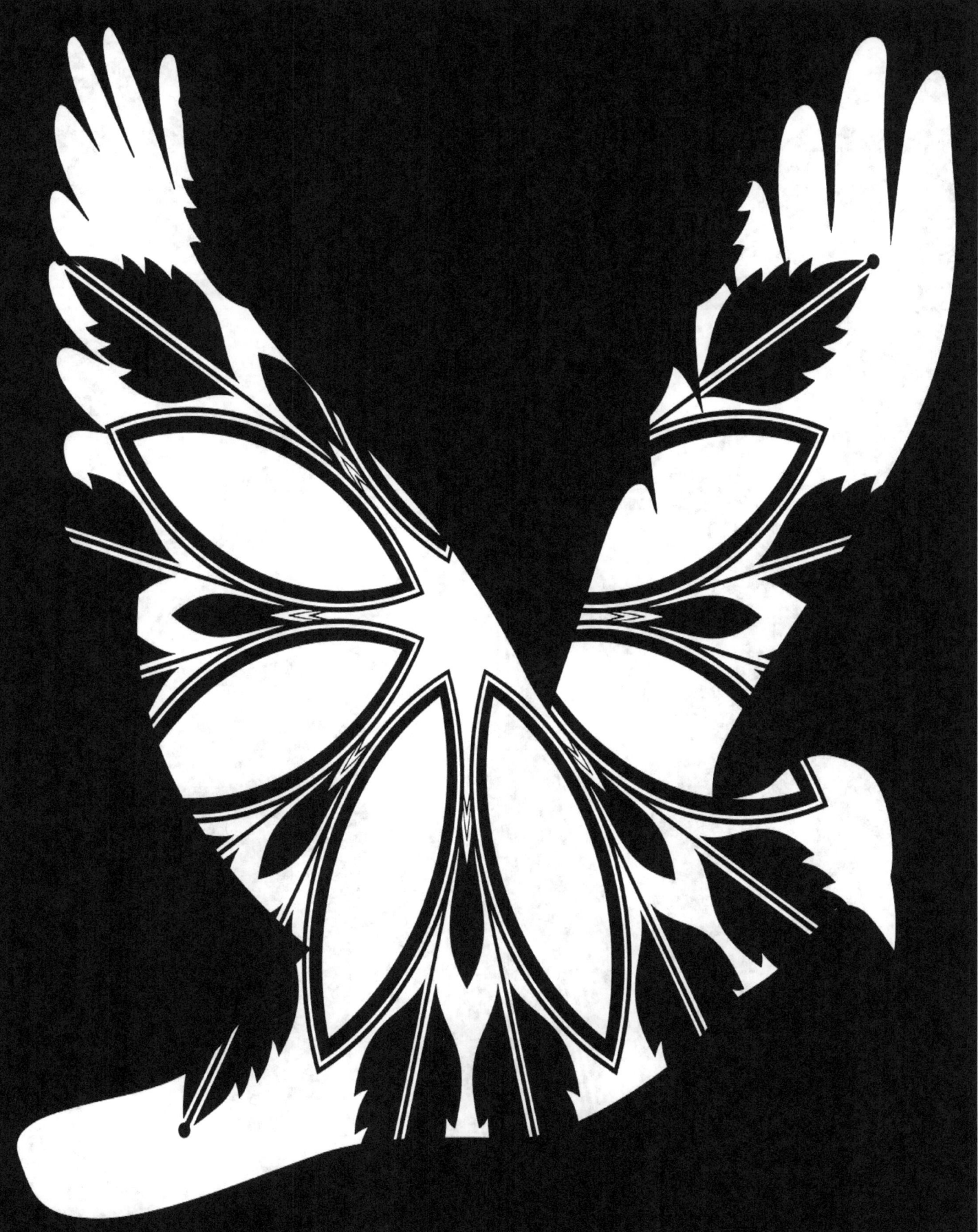

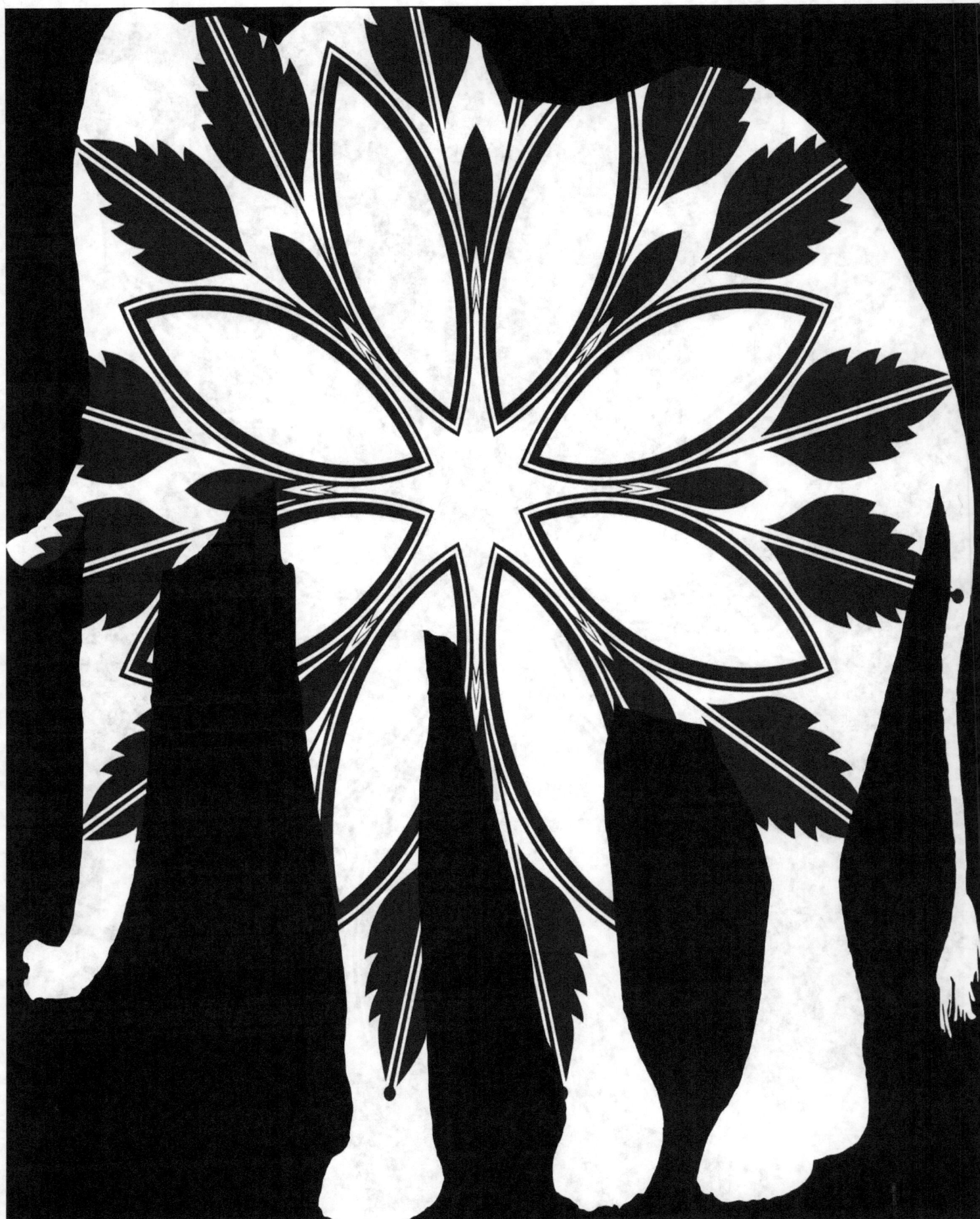

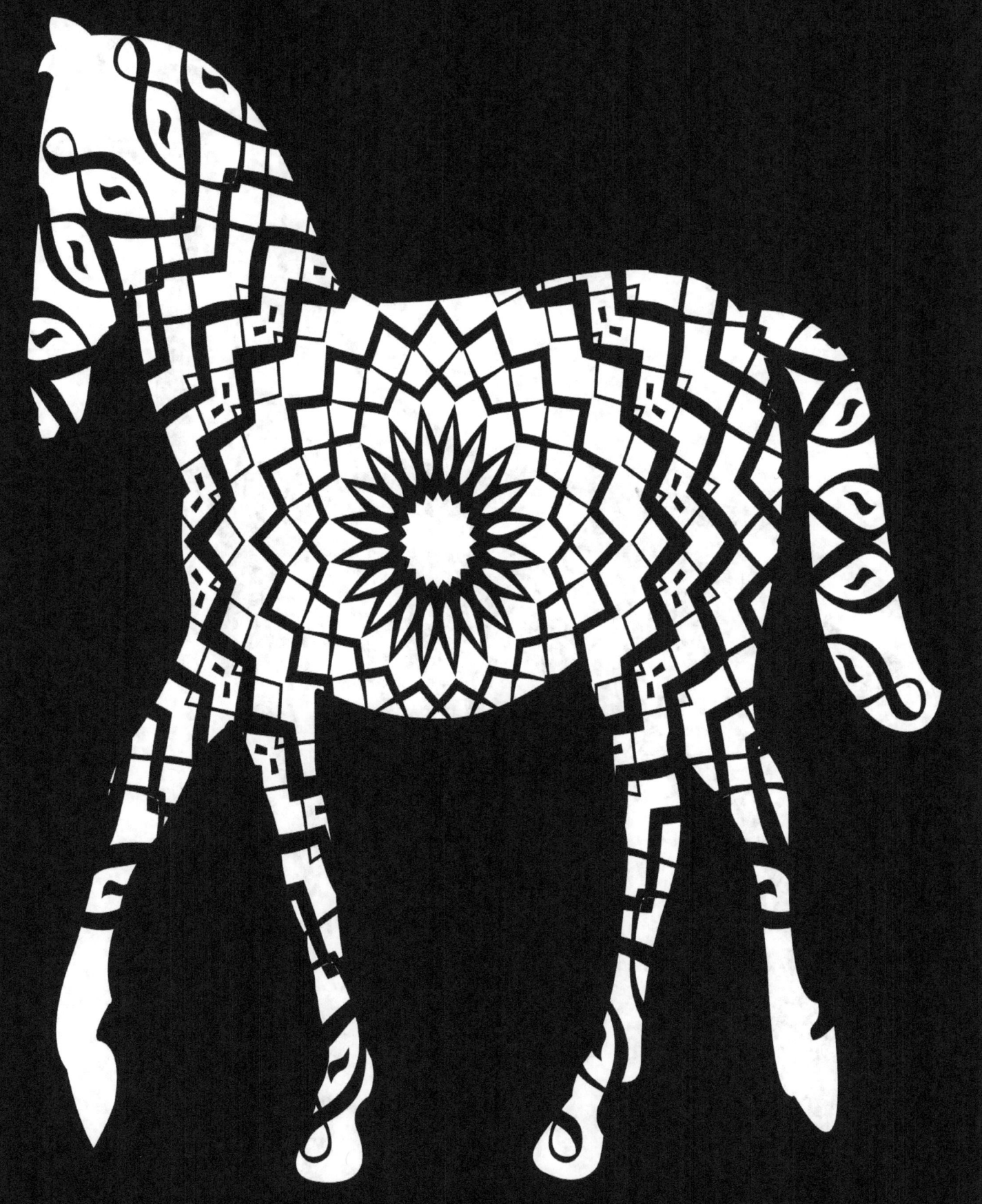

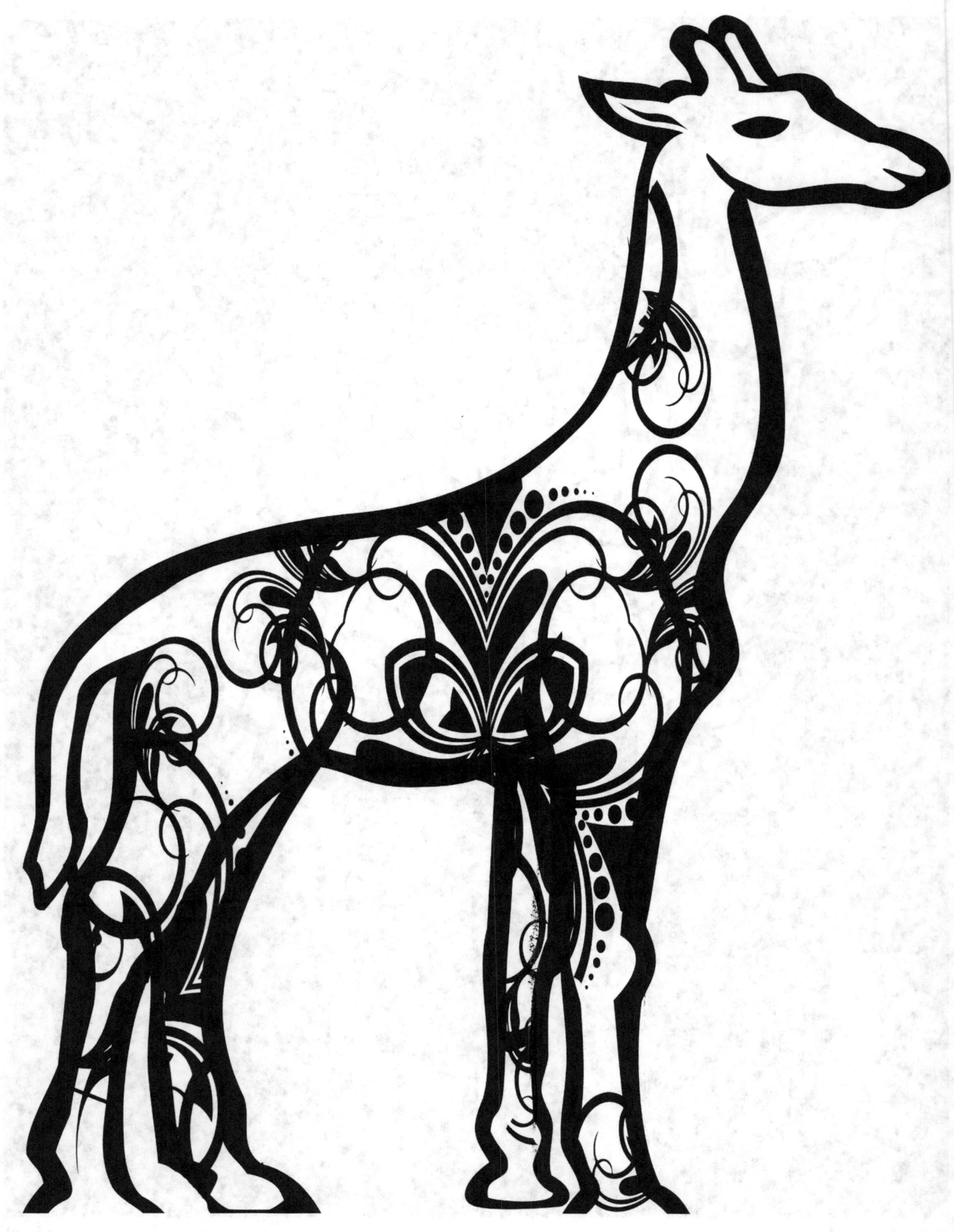

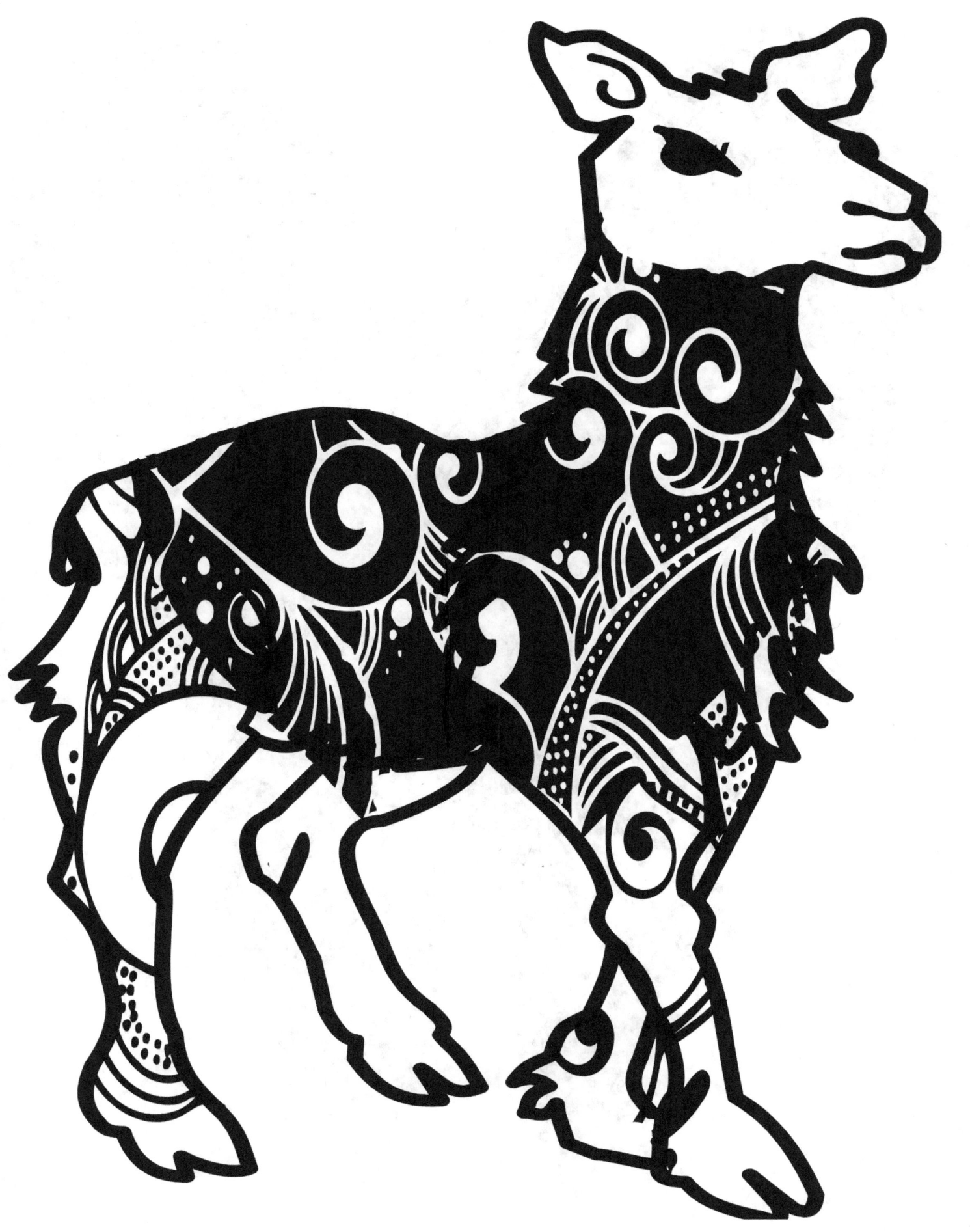

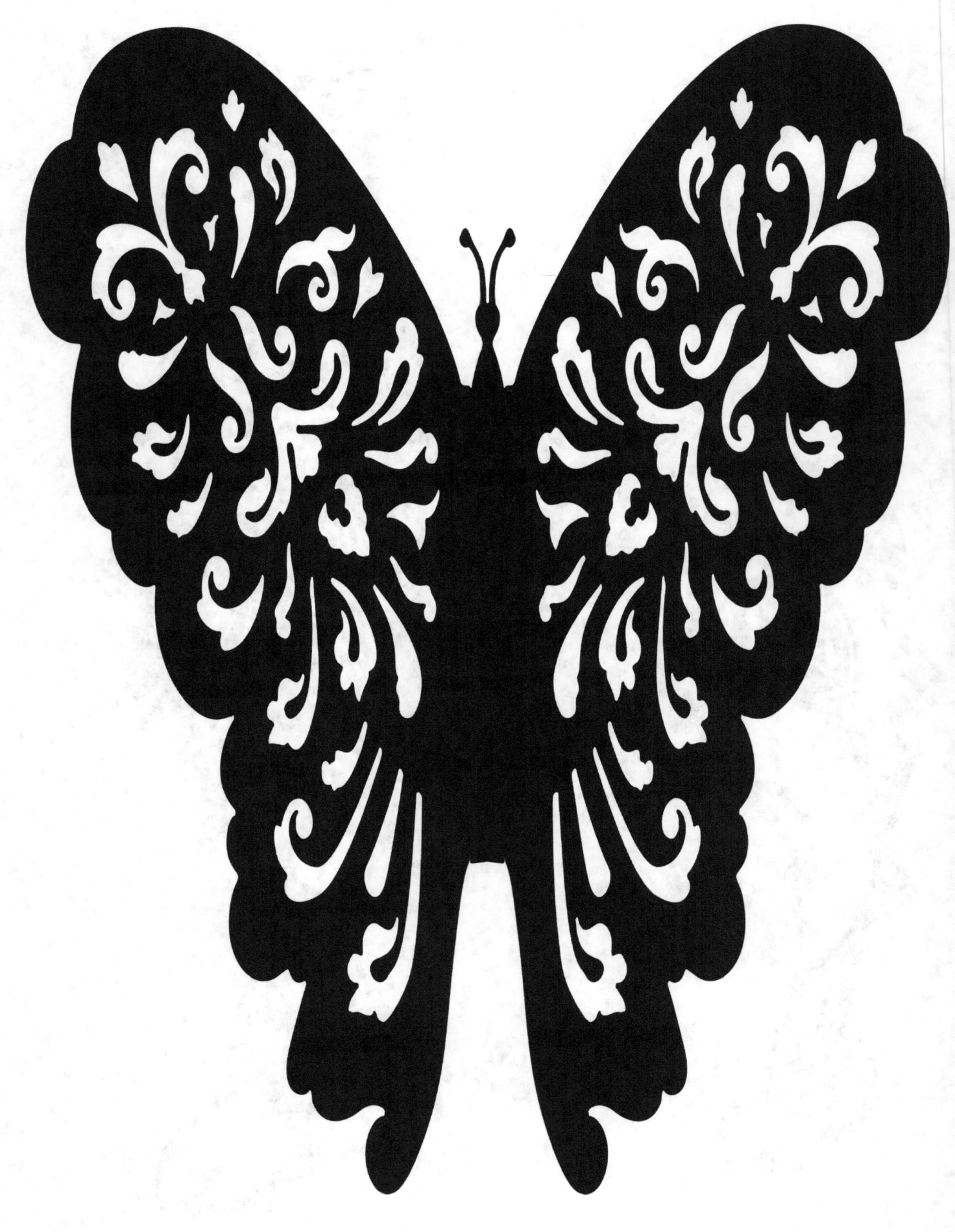

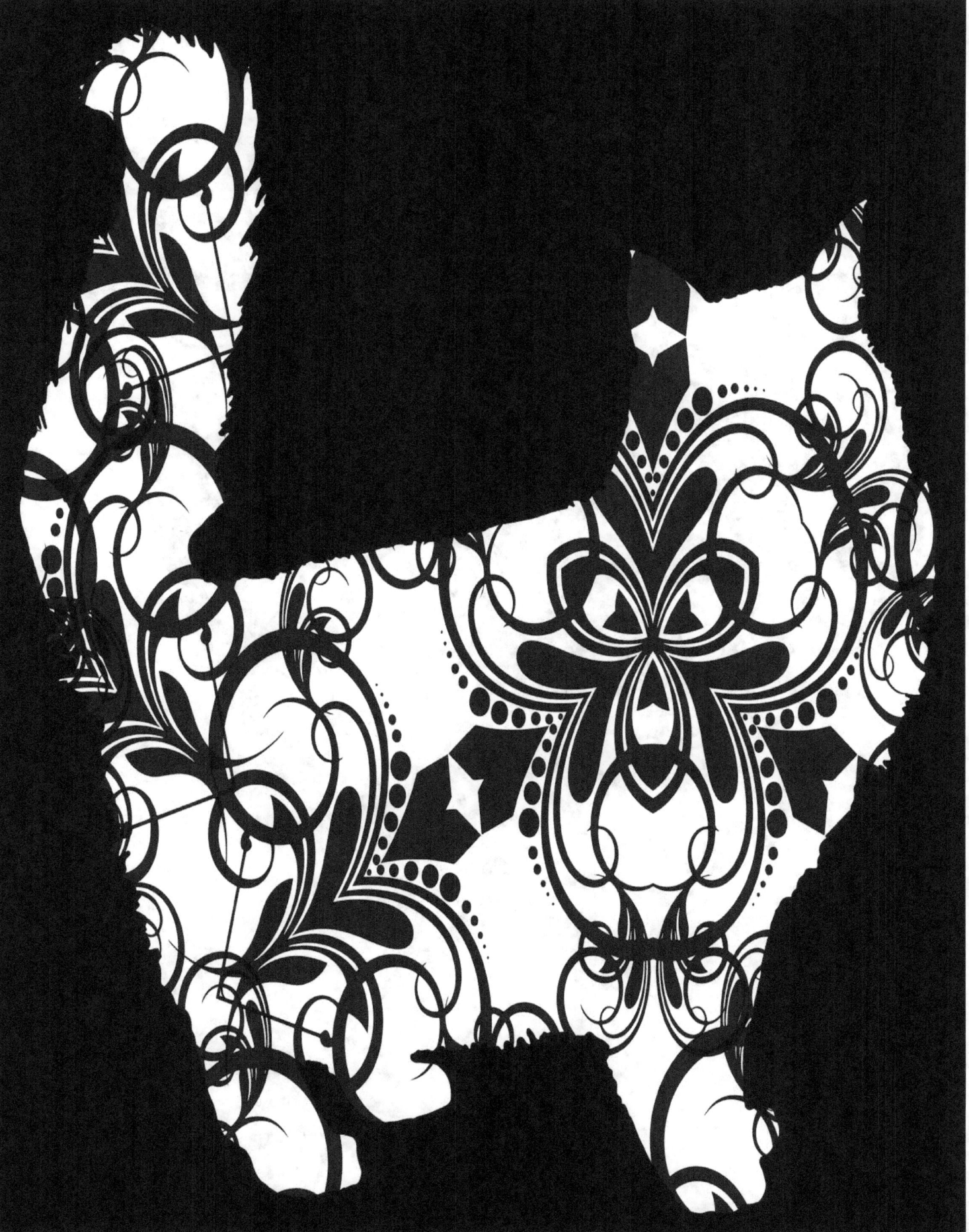

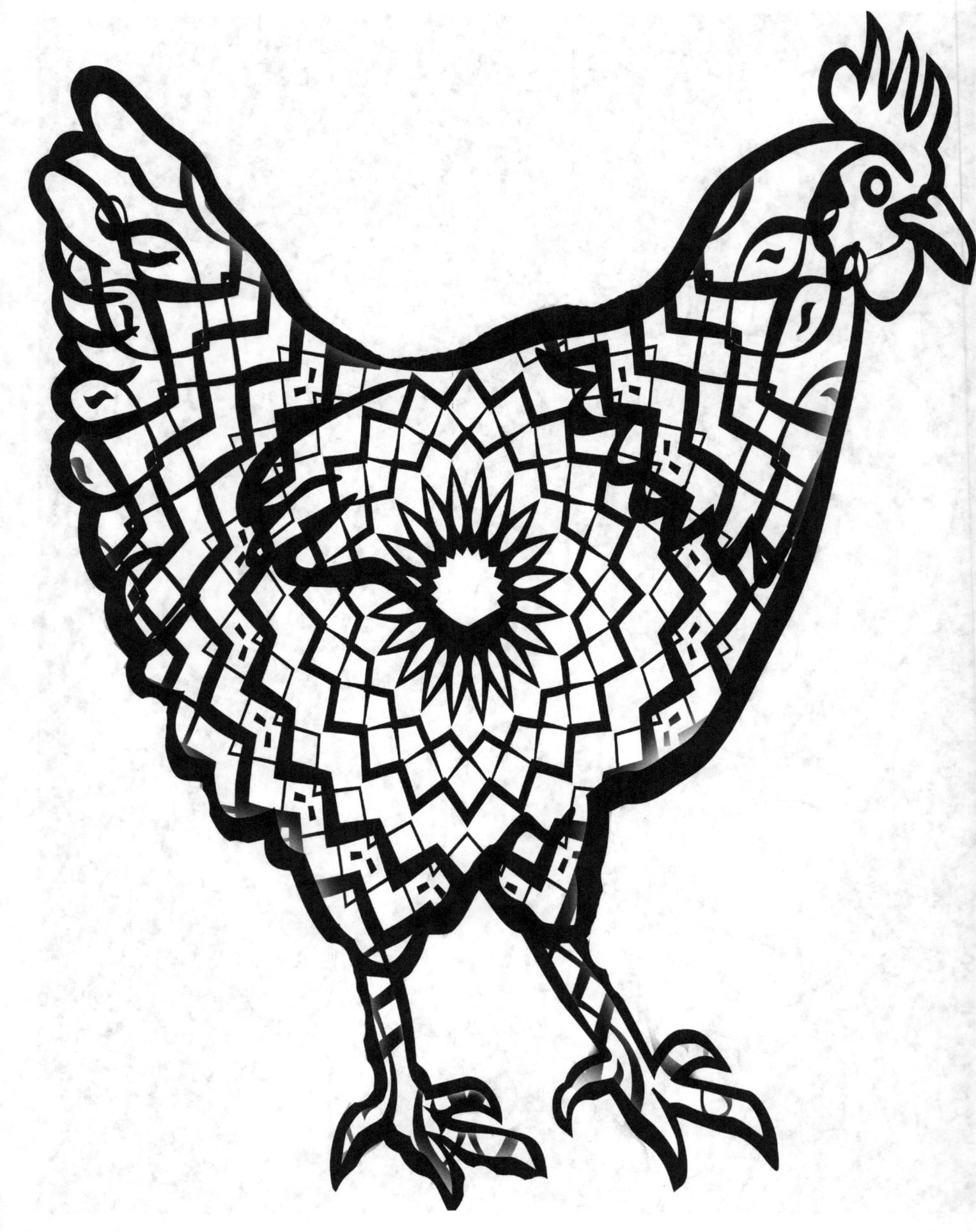

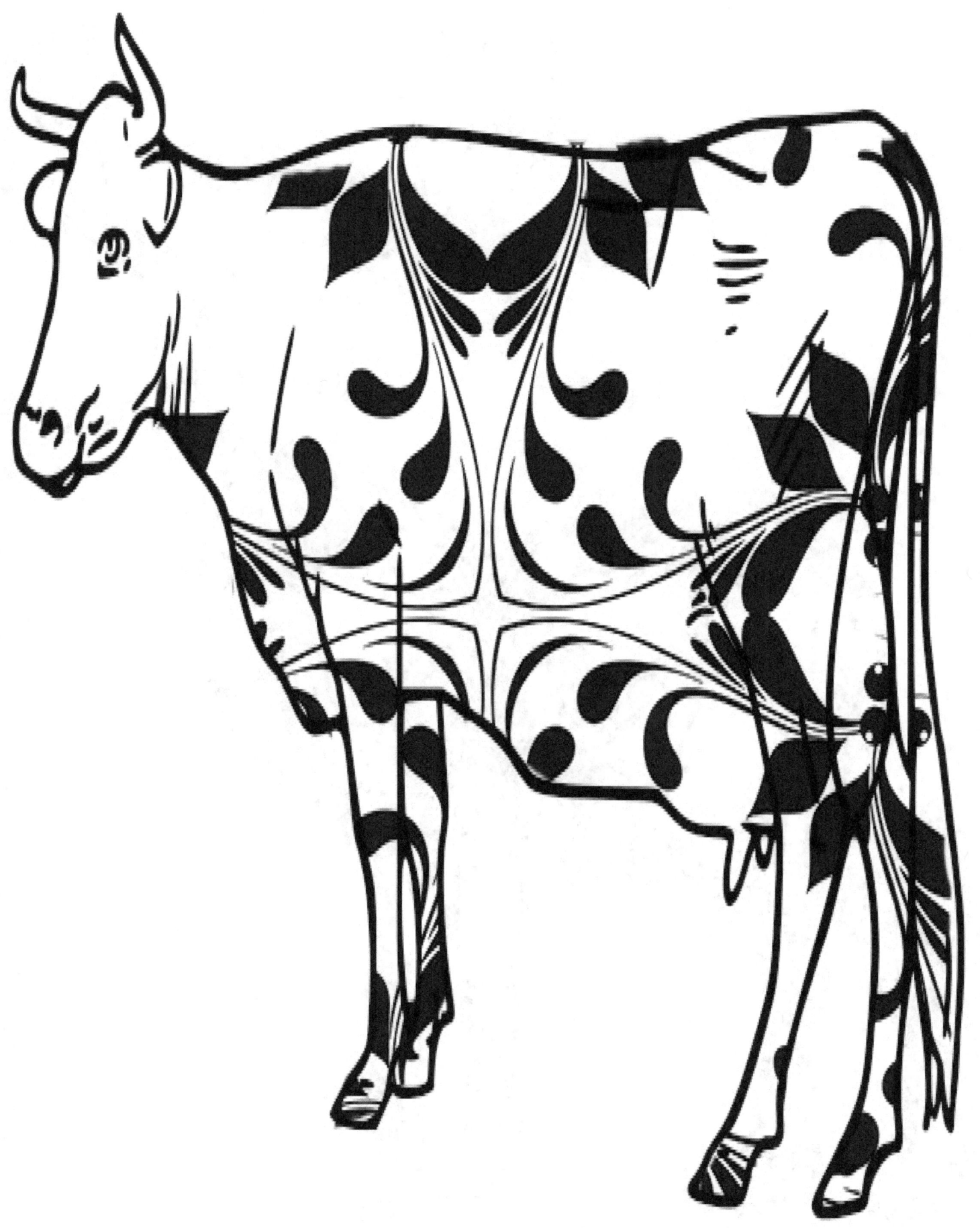

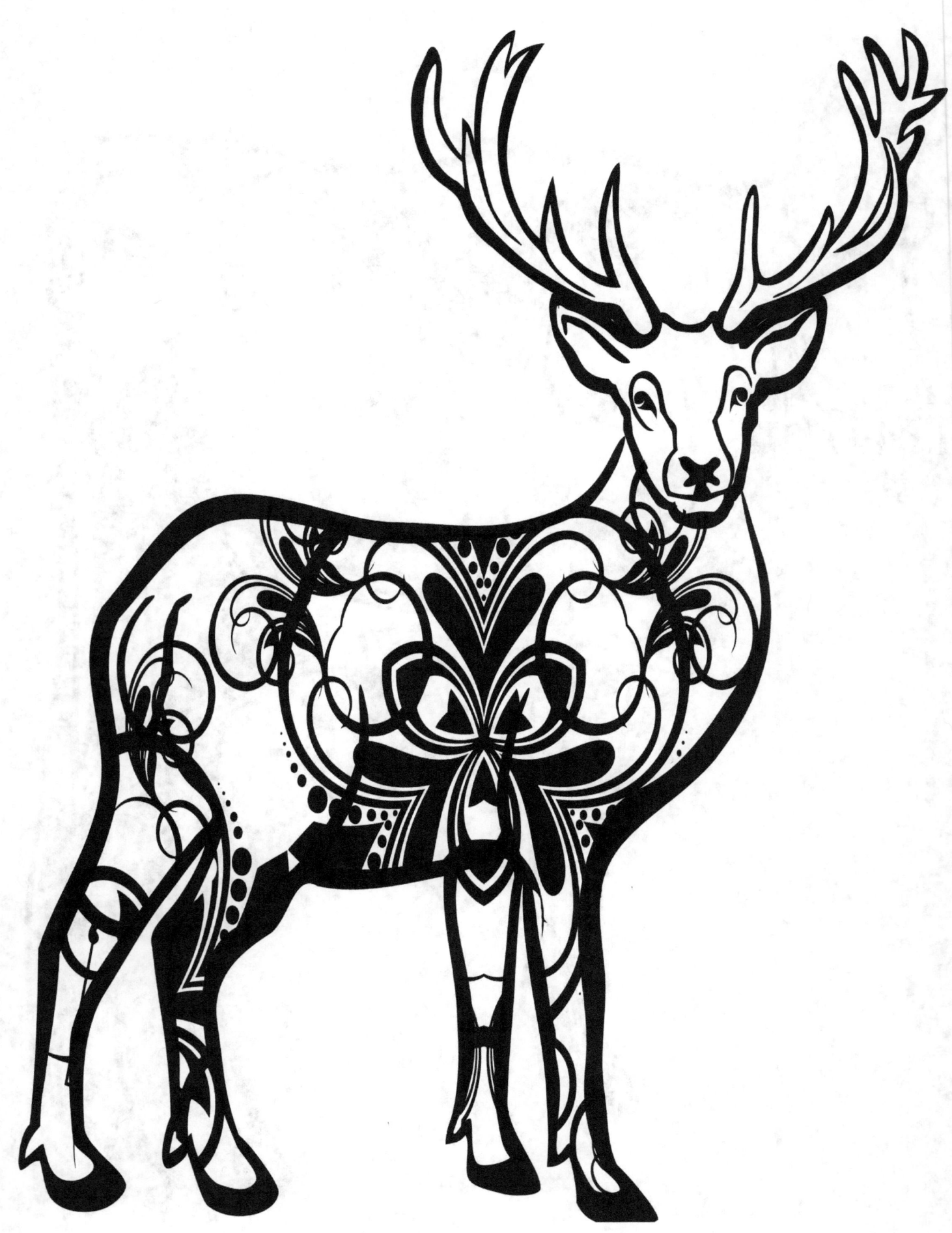

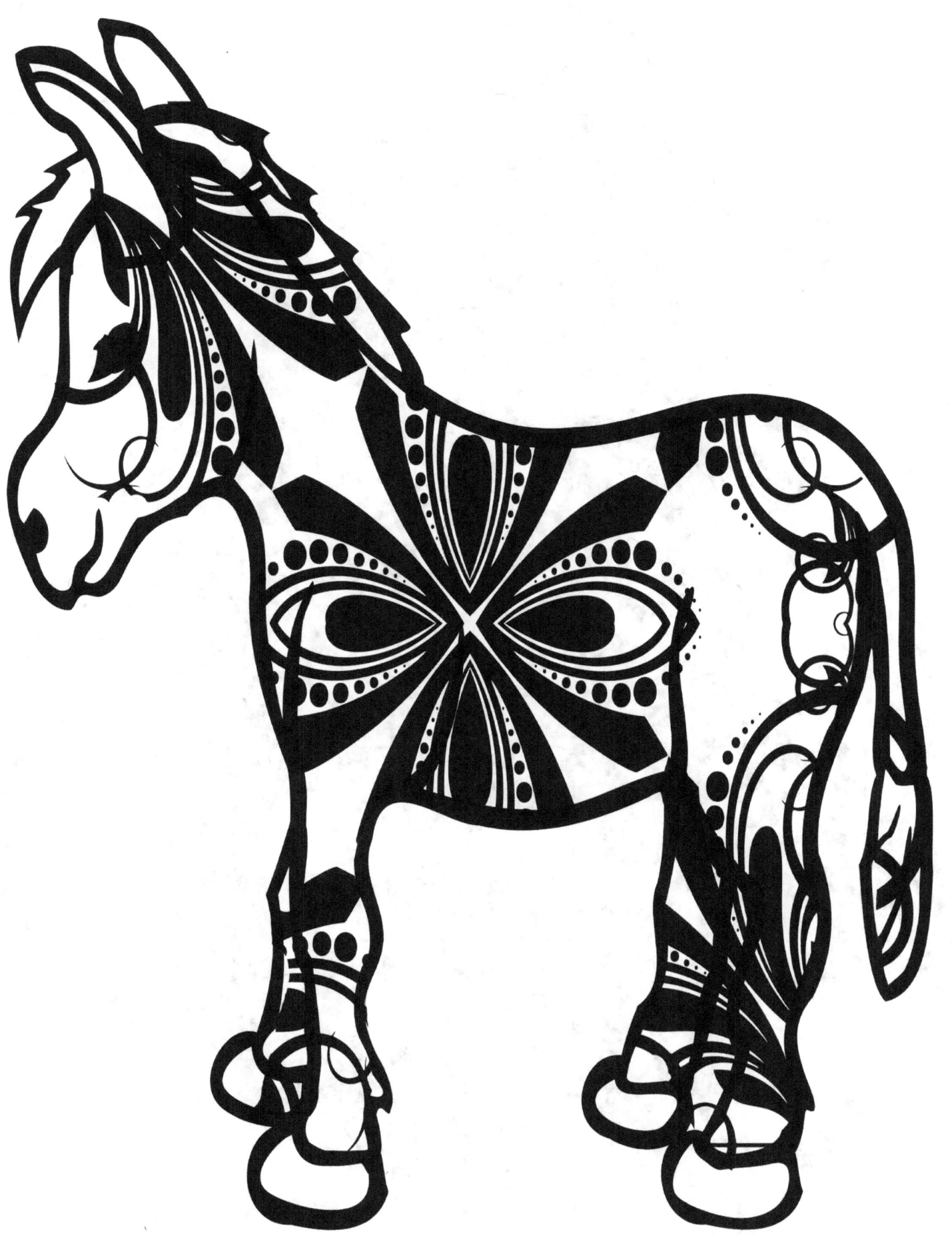

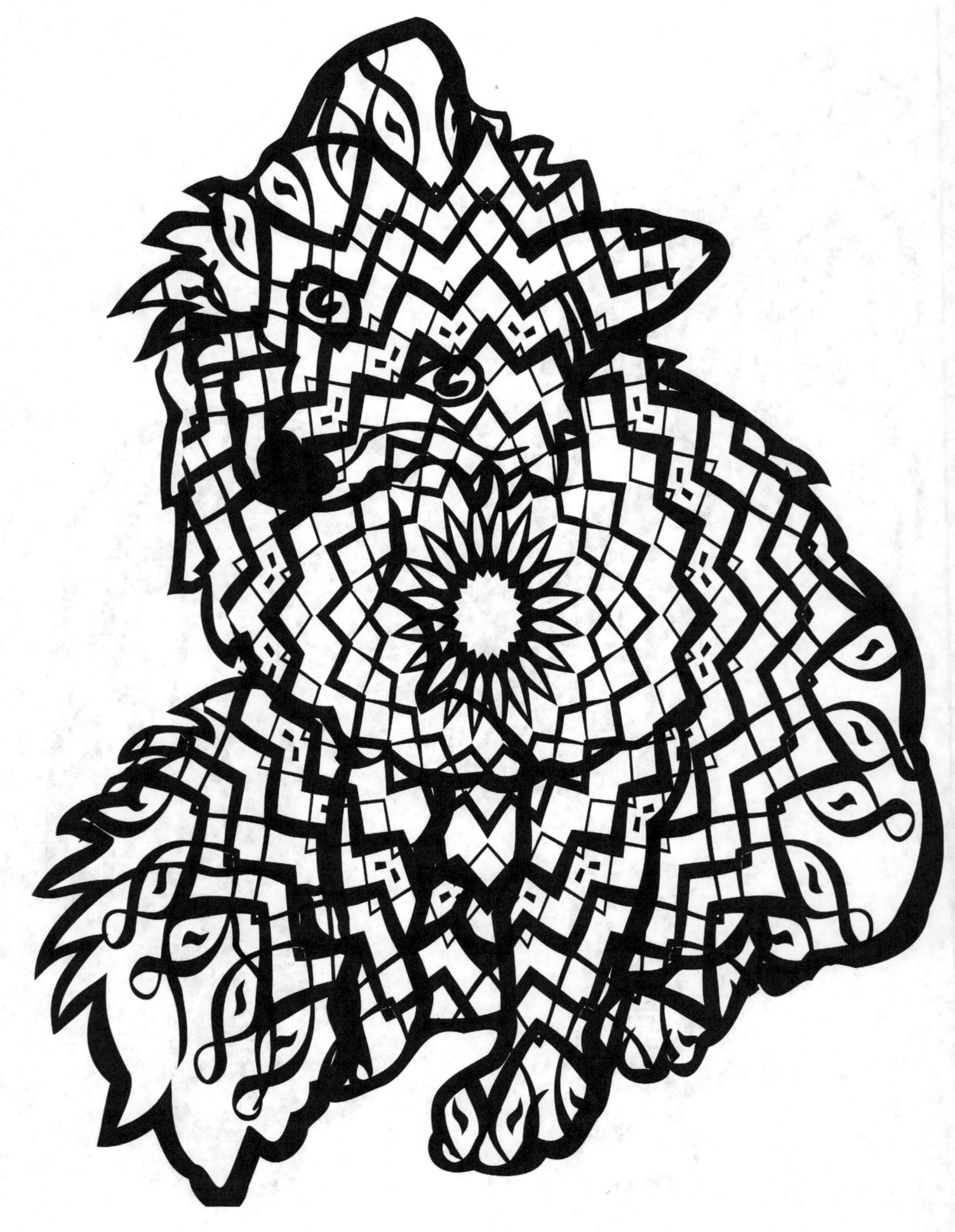

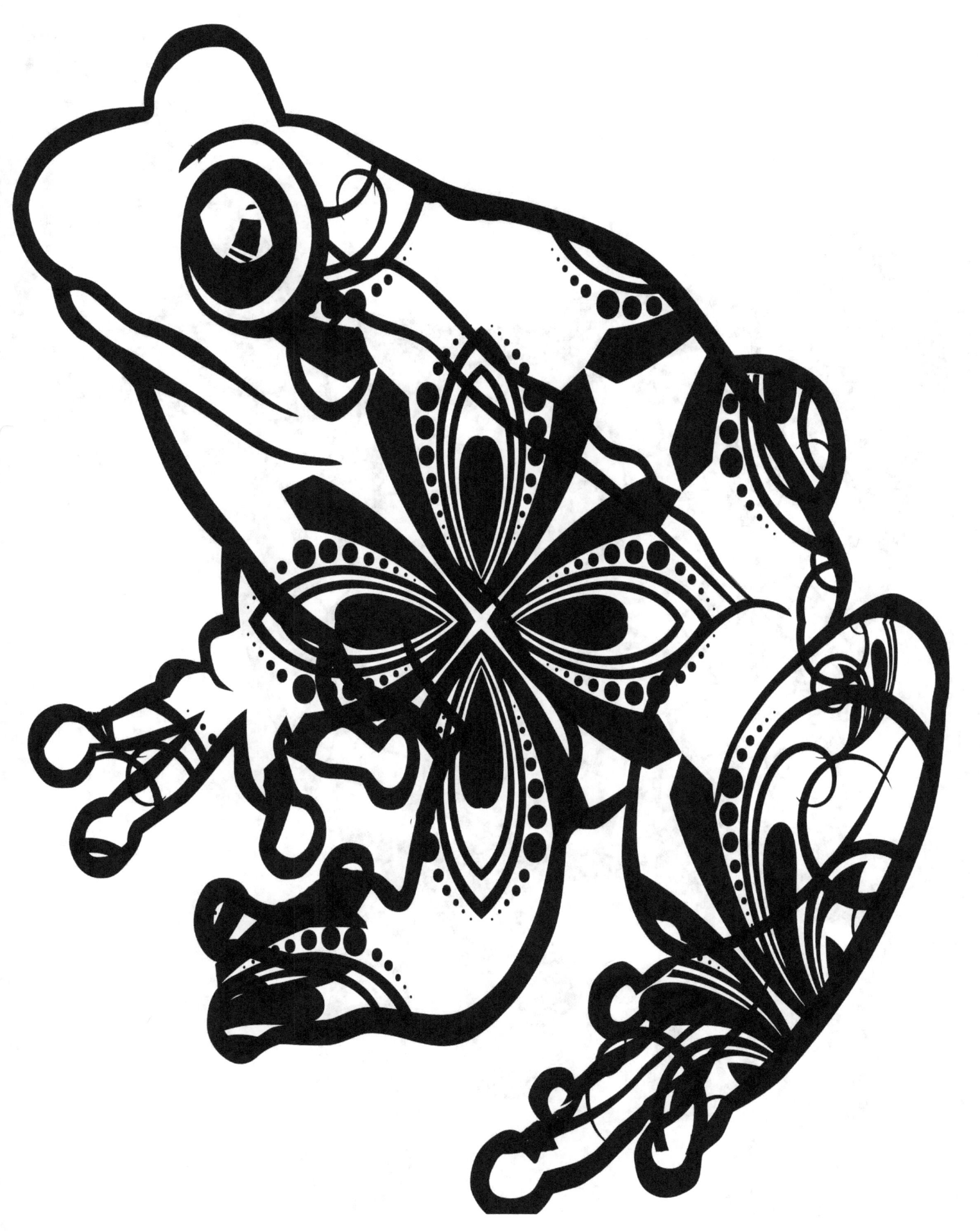

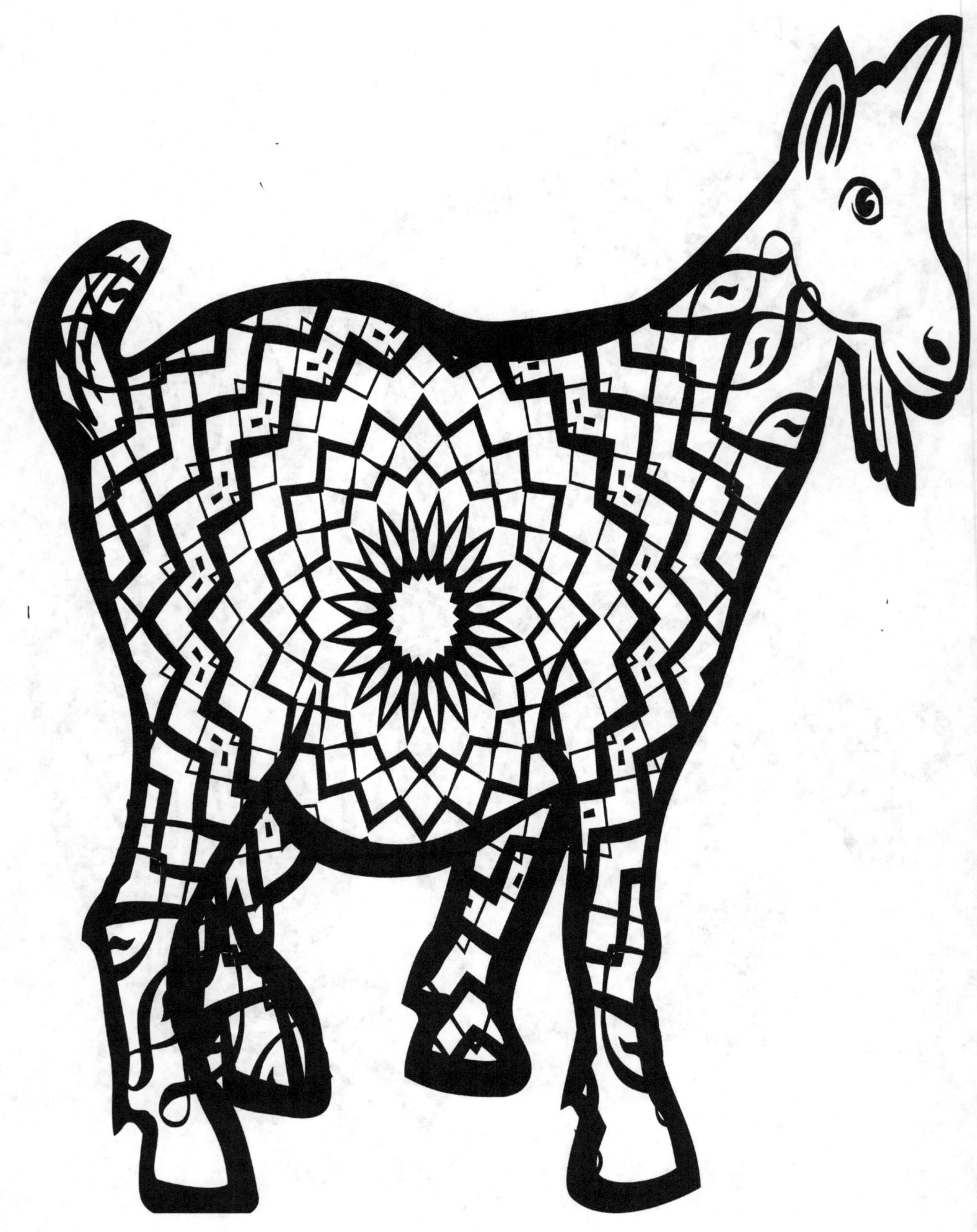

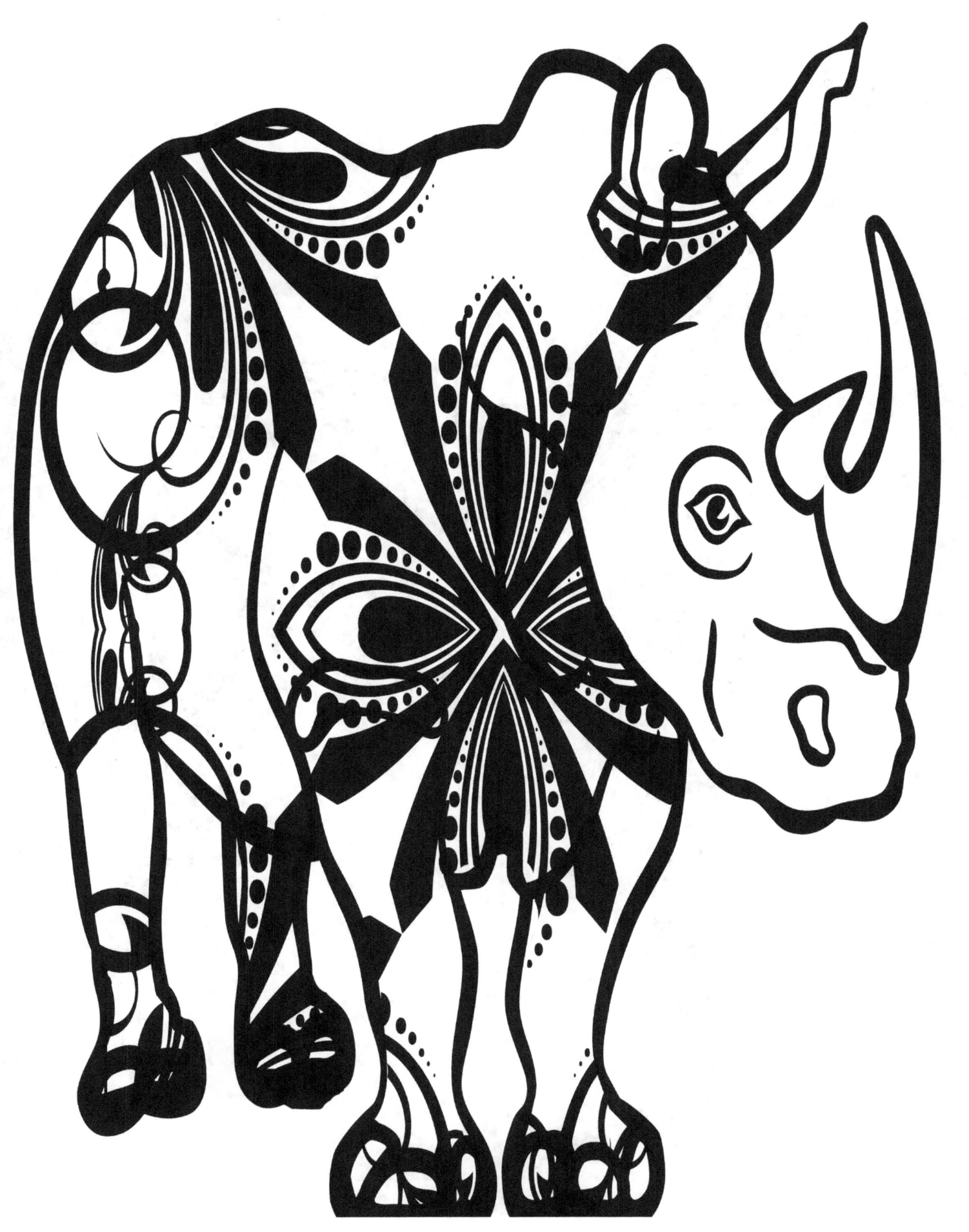

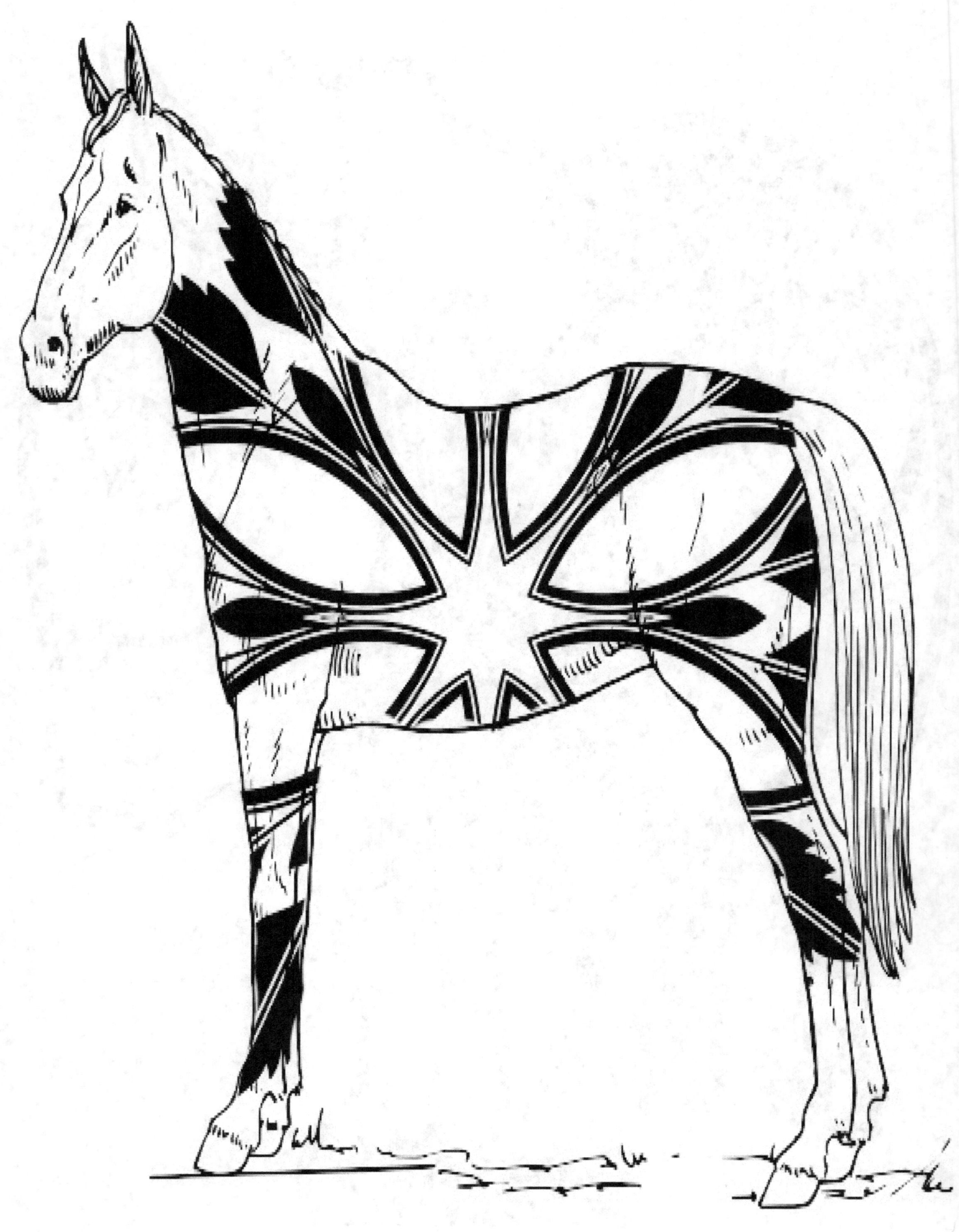

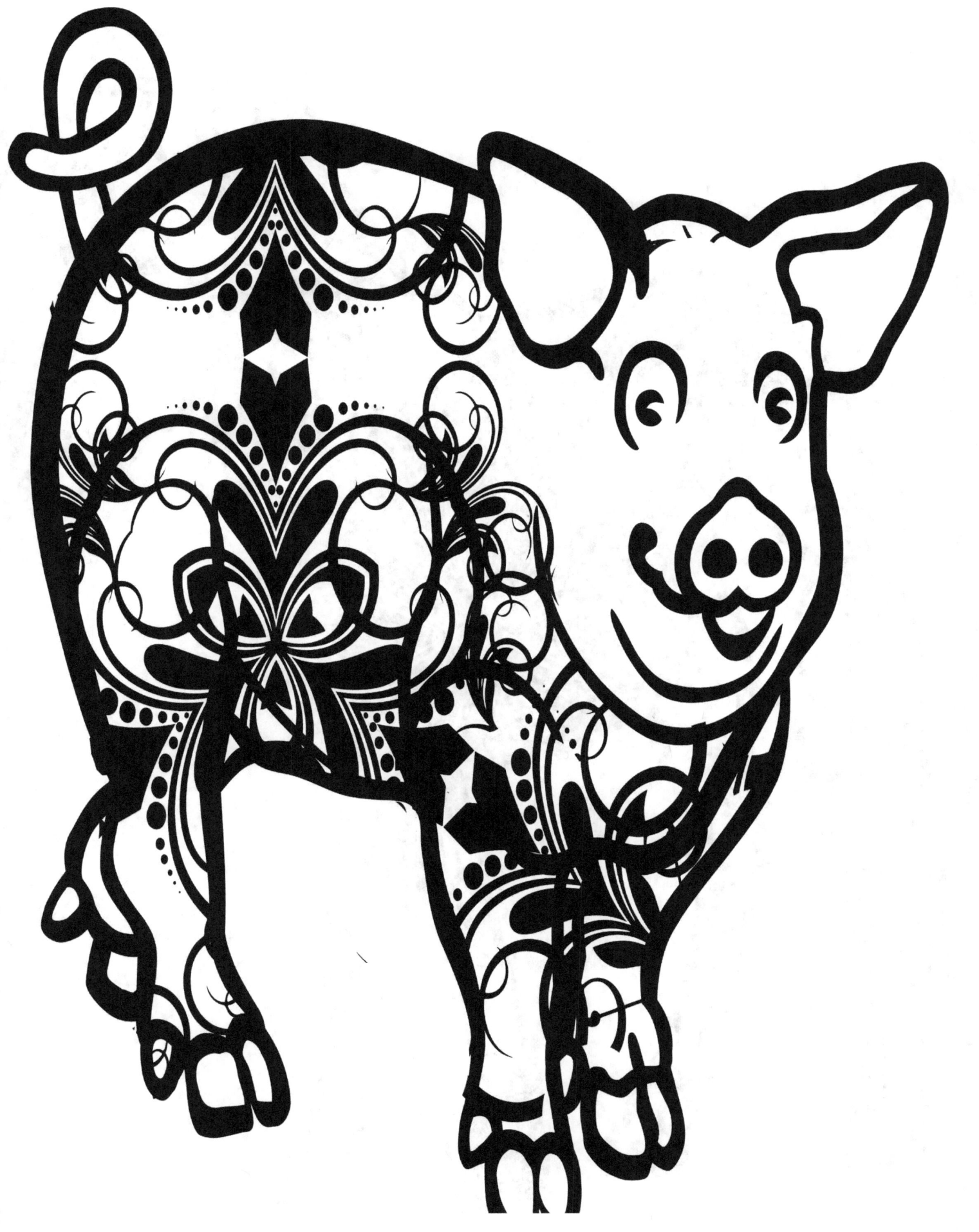

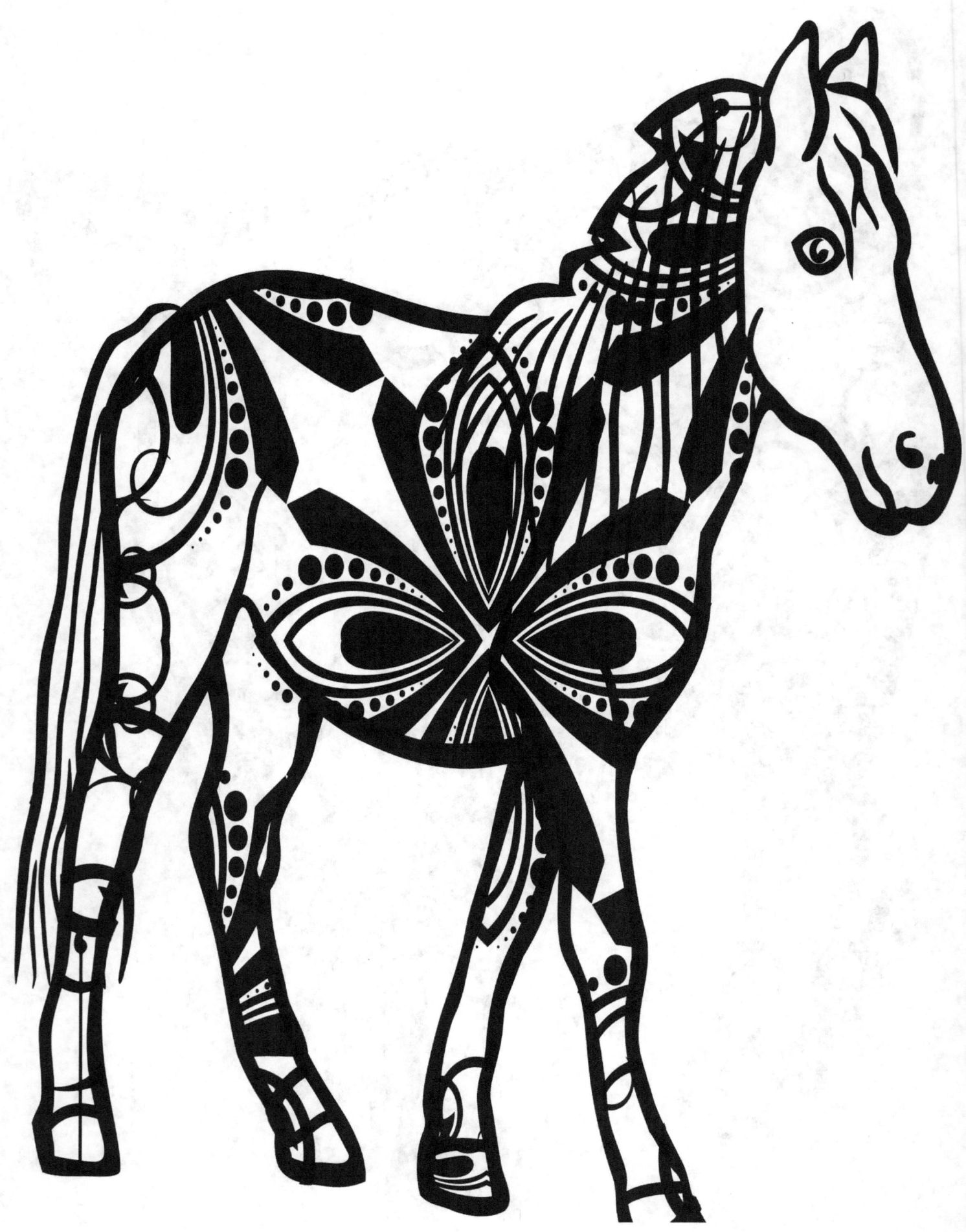

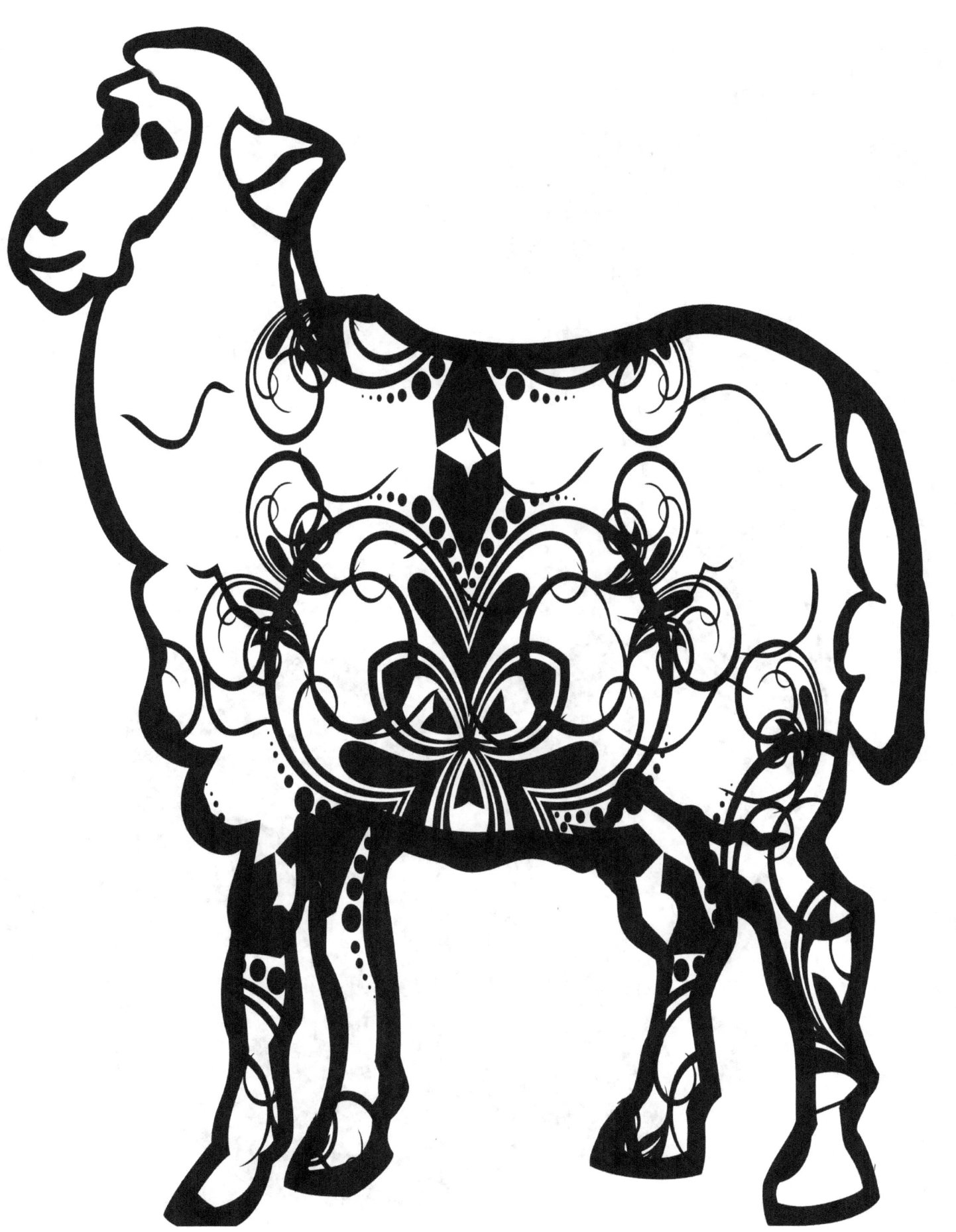

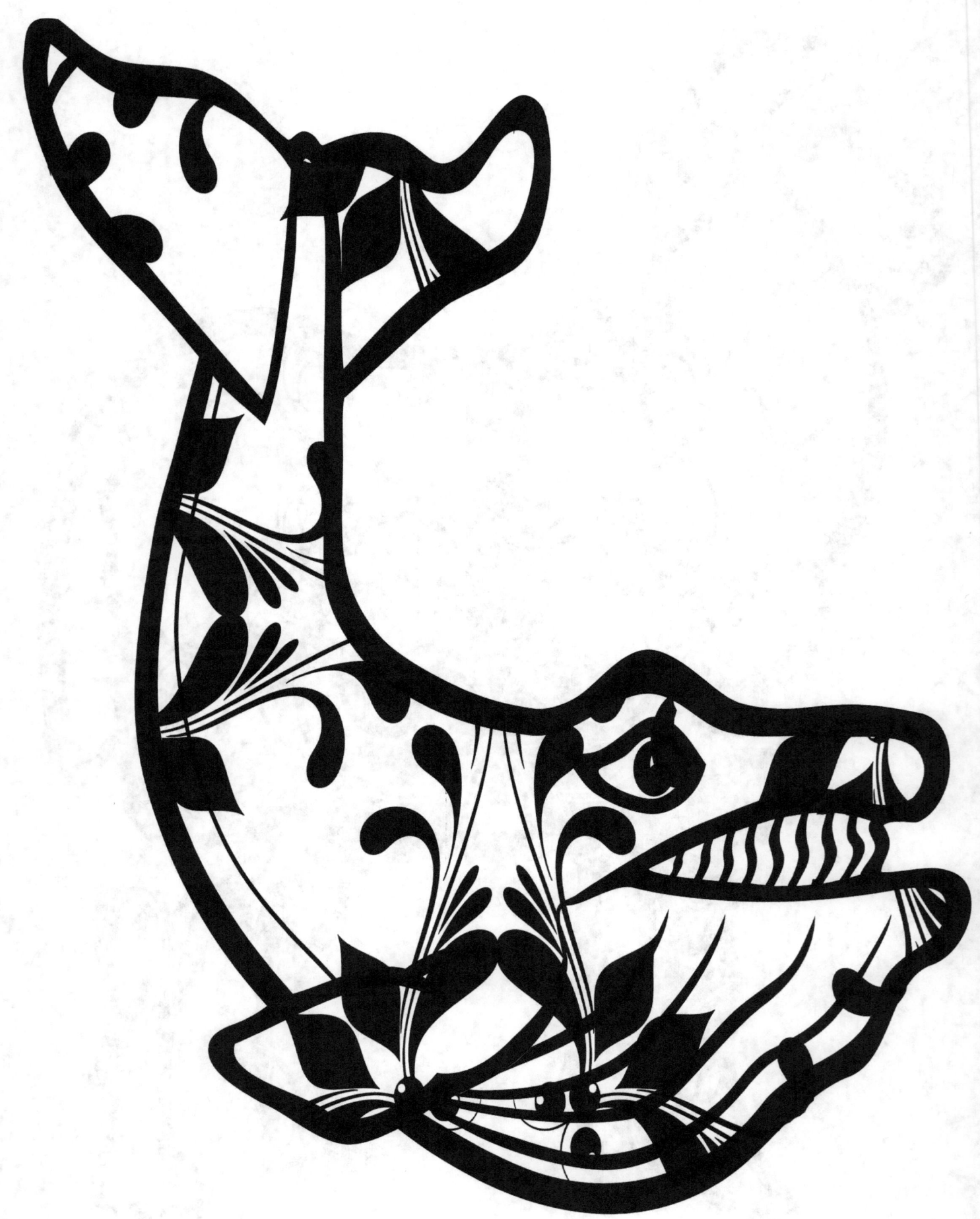

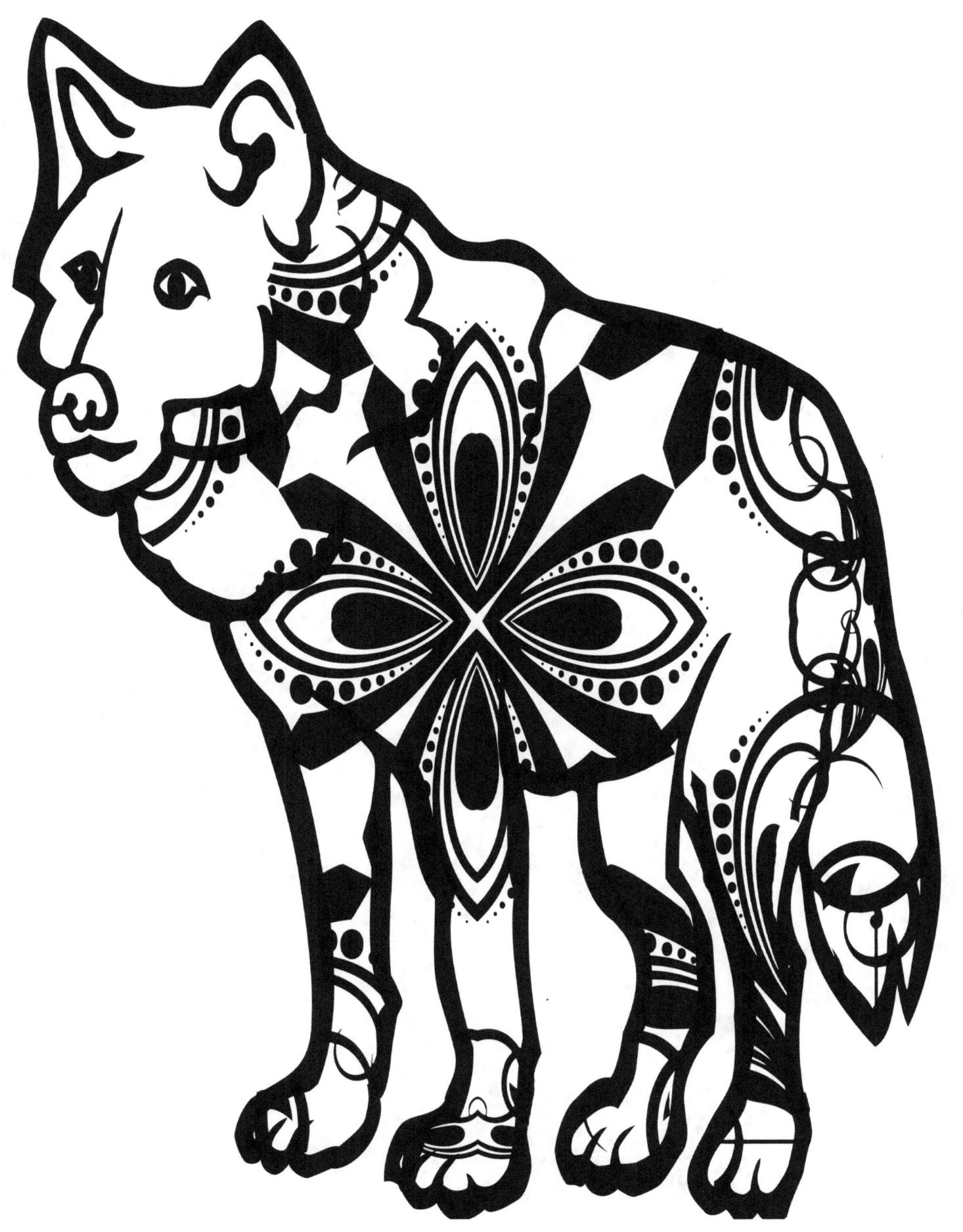

If you like this book, be sure to check out the other Adult Coloring Books we have at:

www.ravenswoodpublishing.com

Thank you for your patronage.

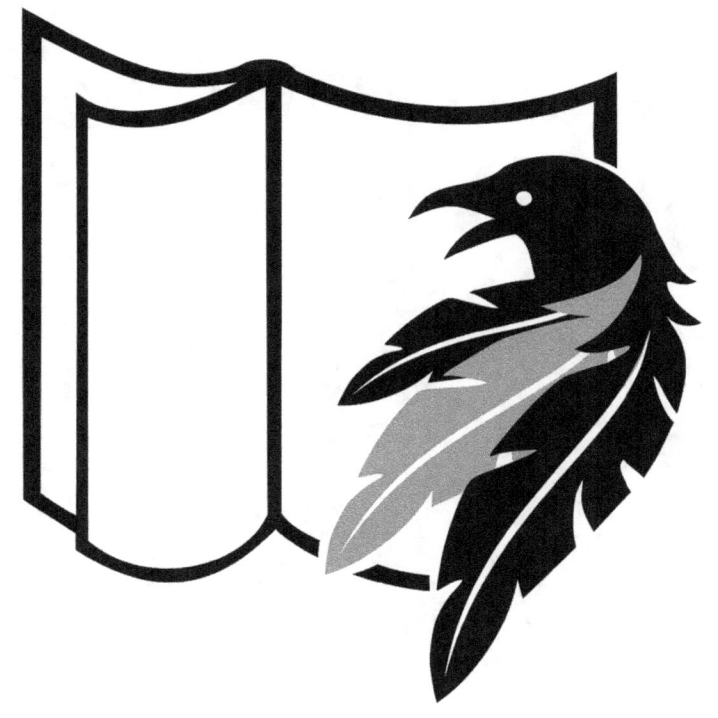